The Unicorn Poem

&

Flowers and Songs
of Sorrow

E. A. Mares

The first version of *The Unicorn Poem* was published by Ernest Tedlock's San Marcos Press, Los Cerrillos, New Mexico, in 1980. Parts of this poem, at times in somewhat different form, appeared in *La Confluencia, Symbiosis Quarterly, Festival de Floricanto, Sunstone Review, New Mexico Magazine,* and *Voices from the Rio Grande.*

Several of the other poems in this edition appeared, sometimes in earlier versions, in *San Marcos Review, Unexpected Events: Poems from Writers in New Mexico, New Mexico Magazine, La Confluencia, Ghost Ranch Journal, Blue Mesa Review, El Cuaderno, The Indian Rio Grande, Voices from the Rio Grande, Resiembra, Southwest: A Contemporary Anthology,* and *Las Vegas, New Mexico: A Portrait.*

First edition, August 1992
ISBN 0-931122-65-1

Cover drawing, *Santa Fe Bar, ca. 1940,* by Edward R. Gonzales
Design by Michael Reed
Typography by Prototype

West End Press • P.O. Box 27334 • Albuquerque, NM 87125

CONTENTS

The Unicorn Poem 1

On Signing an Agreement to Read Poetry
at a State University 23

Juana La Loca 24, 25

Some Reflections in the Desert 26

The Second Coming 27

Bosque, North Valley, Albuquerque 28

Cleofes Vigil 29

Horses 30

News Item 32

Flight of Crows 33

Once a Man Knew His Name 34

Mama Snake 37

In the San Antonio Hotel 38

Flowers and Songs of Sorrow 40

El Perro Mexicano / The Mexican Dog 42, 43

The Day I Fell in Love with Josephine Earp 46

On Reading in a Newspaper that I Am a Star 47

La Coqueta 48

Christmas at the Health Care Center on the West Mesa . . . 50

'38 Chevy 52

Lunch at the Gyros 54

Paula Angel 55

Discourse of the Severed Head of Joaquín Murieta 56

Dialogue with a Skull Found in Las Vegas, New Mexico . . . 58

On a Photograph by Alex Traube 60

Trusting the Fire Not To Go Out 61

From Las Vegas Journal 62

The Road to Fenton Lake 64

Command Prompt 65

Poem [in memory of Jim Hall] 66

Elegy for Ramon Sender 67

Watching Old Movies 68

On an Edward R. Gonzales Drawing
of a Santa Fe Bar, Circa 1940 70

Afterword by Angel Gonzalez 72, 73

This book is dedicated to
Ernesto, Maria, Galit, Vered,
My children,
To give them words of love,
Traces of memory,
Shadows of people
Who were as real and insubstantial
As ourselves, as words.

THE UNICORN POEM

On Seeing a Detailed Map
of Old Town, Albuquerque

I notice the empty space
where there is no map,
only theater of man and myth,

where there is no path
to the wild mesas,
the shimmering fields of the unicorn,

a great land of dream and memory,
where less lovely beasts pursue
and try to corral him.

El unicornio
malherido por la cadena que rompió
y el coral puntiagudo
que saltó, corre por los campos
rumbo a . . .
los sueños y el recuerdo.
Ya vienen los perros.
El unicornio sangra, sangra.
Se vuelve pura espuma del sufrir,
un leve humo blanco.
Se vuelve pura esperanza.

The unicorn,
badly wounded
by the chain he broke
and the sharp-tipped picket fence he jumped,
runs through the fields
toward . . .
dreams and memory.
The unicorn bleeds, bleeds.
He becomes the lather of suffering,
a thin white smoke.
He becomes a pure hope.

To the east are the Sandia Mountains
where Apaches hidden by time
look down on the great city
stretching far to the west
and all along the Rio Grande valley.

They are beyond the old pain now,
the shrinking land and the suffocating sky.
Once in a while they recall
the good times and as a jest
they send a bear
scampering down into Albuquerque
to test the state of laughter
there on the asphalt streets,
the surface of the smoothed-over rift.

Enormous caterpillars called "Eucs"
have cut a swath
across the Sandias
gouging deeper than any book
has ever made a furrow
through my mind.

Tourists speed by
perhaps not sensing the scar tissue,
the plowed-up land,
not likely to see the aspen,
cedar, deer and wild goat
above the limestone ledge.

It is not where logic and tools
conspire to simplify the land
that a poem
snares the fish of light
in a shadowed stand of pine.

I choose the forest
and the peaks behind my eyes
above the road cut,
where a hobbled unicorn cries
and a white whale breeches
through El Greco's tumbling skies.

From these heights
the city down below forms a bowl
whose center is Old Town;
not the make-believe Old Town,
the Hollywood Old Town,
but rather as it was then called,
Alburquerque,
where it all began

in the unhurried nights and days
a long time ago,
where the small ranches
spread out along the river
and slowly the plaza formed
a diminutive stage,
the center of my universe.

Boxes on the map
are meant to be houses
made of words.
Discrete squares,
loops and rectangles
form this world of ink.
It would become cluttered, messy,
to try to show the details
inside the make-believe worlds
these lines on paper represent.
Straight lines suddenly veer
or curve to follow some unknown contour
of the mind or of the land.

They are roads made of words
obscure as the kingdom
from which they come.

En el reinado de la palabra
todo puede ser.
El rey absurdo ni apenas
se vista de tinta.
Los vasallos andan por allá
entre las sílabas.
Y los demás,
es decir el pueblo,
como es ahora
y siempre ha sido,
forma el fondo oscuro
del reinado de la palabra.

In the kingdom of the word
everything is possible.
The absurd king is not even barely
dressed in ink.
His vassals scurry around
through the syllables.

And the rest,
that is to say, the people,
as it is now and always has been,
form the obscure backdrop
for the kingdom of the word.

Roads are words
leading to

silence

where the map falters,
becomes the screechy note on the violin,
the musician blinded by the desert sun,

where the map stumbles
into a whiteness
as total as death.

He cruzado caminos
en los sueños.
Caminos que dan a la muerte.
El letrero de un camino dice "Roma,"
pero a Roma llegan
muy pocos caminos de aquí.

Son caminos
que se parecen mucho
a los caminos despiertos.

Son caminos
donde hay poca gente.
Caminos que dan a un parque
o a una vega placentera
en medianoche
con un jardín que pronto se hace
camposanto
con cruces
bajo luz blanca,
y todo esto
envuelto en la niebla que lleva
el barco del sueño.

Todo mar y camino
llegan al margen
de la nada
donde no hay ni huella que seguir.

Aquí el poeta con su pluma
dibuja imágenes
de su porvenir.

In dreams
I have come upon roads
leading to death.
A road sign says "Roma,"
but few roads here
lead to Rome.

These dream roads
are very much like wide awake
roads.

These are roads
with few people,
roads leading to a park,
the pleasant meadow
at midnight
and there is a garden
that changes into a cemetery
with crosses
bathed in white light.
And all this happens
wrapped in the fog carrying
the ghost ship of dreams along.

All roads and seas
lead to the edge
of nothingness
where not even a clue
is left to follow.
Here the poet with his pen
sketches out images
for his future.

Inside the boxes
there is an incessant whirl.
People and their possessions
seek form,
the ultimate solidity of words.

Long before there were words,
the curious tracks they leave
across an empty space,

the only map
was in the eye of the eagle
gliding along the canyon walls,
or in the fine particles of sand
forming an undulating S,
the wake of the serpent
sidewinding its way south
beneath this sun.

Once people formed by the light
became Aztecs wandering this land.
Their lips uttered words
and the words became gods.
Ometecuhtli and Omecihuatl,
Lord and Lady of Our Sustenance.
Quetzalcoatl,
God of Life,
Creator of the People,
Lord of the House of Dawn.
Tezcatlipoca,
omnipotent God of Darkness,
God of Sorcerers and Highwaymen,
Lord of the House of Night.

We are not the Aztecs
who left ghost trails here.
We remember them.
We are the victims
of all the Aztecs—
Mexican Aztecs
Spanish Aztecs
Anglo Aztecs
Pick Your Own Favorite Aztecs.

We are the sacrificed
in this land
where the Lord of the House of Night
grows fat
at the Feast of the Flaying of Men.
Reluctantly, we leave home and wander.

Sometimes our barrios
recall the family names of founders—
los Barelas, Martineztown,
los Candelarias—or the saints—

San José, San Felipe—
and we remember them
on our travels
for we constantly move about
and we are far from Aztlán.

We travel with the circus,
the high-wire artists,
the clowns, sideshow barkers,
sellers of popcorn and cotton candy,
on the back roads through country towns.
Listen to the creaking wheels,
the caravan's groan.
See the dust
where our tents rise
in Old Town.
There is always one more show
and we are far from Aztlán.

Words become seeds of maize
the healing herbs of the medicine man.
Words become mud villages
named with the flint edge
of cliff, wind, and star.
Tiguex, Alcanfor, Isleta, Sandia.

Spaniards brought their words
for the shapes of horses, sheep,
metal plows, swords and crosses,
wheat, apples, peaches.
Franciscans offered up
their sales pitch—
sin, forgiveness, salvation,
the trade-in offer for the old
native gods.

Clouds of ivory
tinge the Spanish sky,
burst and fall in Mozarabic light,
a fountain spray
beneath al Andaluz sun
caught in some Alhambran
garden of my mind.

Evening toward Africa
and a dark muezzin

calls down the Moorish night
to the narrow streets of Granada.
Golden Age ballads
and a song
in praise of wine
by Samuel Ha-Nagid
drift through the olive trees
toward the sea.

Here an occasional Marrano
paused on the journey north,
seeing the Sandias,
seeing Granada in his mind,
and continued on up the valley.

Spanish tongues
fleshed out the bare bones
of love and hate.
Indio
Mestizo
Español
Mexicano
Americano
whispered
the ritual words,
then parted the blessed thighs

In the name of the Father
and of the Son
who will be born of this union . . .
and of the Holy Ghost,
him, the spooky one,
the inscrutable tongue of fire
who threatened to burn me as a child.
Him, the ghost who may have been
the howling birth of strong men and women
who built
la Plaza de Alburquerque,
the Church of San Felipe Neri,
ad majorem gloriam dei.

Words of ancestors
spoke of fabulous islands and beasts,
fountains of youth,
cities of gold and heavenly utopias

where the saints would wait
for the second coming of Christ.

Words of ancestors
spoke of Hummingbird-on-the-Left,
an eagle devouring the hearts of men,
the sun who did battle with darkness
and arose every morning
from the pool of night,
human blood and tears.

Word of ancestors
spoke of Jesucristo and his mother,
la Virgen María, who intercedes
with God the Father
to have mercy on sinners.

Sephardic laments
of a lost tribe
carried the words of ancestors
who longed for Zion.

Words of ancestors
sprouted from the lips of the dying,
gathered and hovered
over the rites of extreme unction
and the return to the camposanto.

From where it no longer is,
a star takes aim like a sharpshooter
right at my eyes.

Light scatters in all directions,
a pack of wolves on fire
running to the past and the future.

Bones walk through my shadow
and my body explodes
into a longing for wings.

Coyotes gather in the dark place
circling my path with cold fire.
I cannot answer their hungry jaws.

A bird, a hawk, is a shadow
circling my future,
is carved into stone I cannot see.

Camposanto of words
uncoupling from flesh,
camposanto of words
seeking the lips of a lover,
camposanto of words
unmoved by time
scattering the tombstones,
camposanto of words
crystalline for the moon
fleeting and hard
as an obsidian butterfly,
camposanto of words
you yearn for a song.

The land is stark in New Mexico.
The sky comes right down to the ground
and stamps hard on the earth
insistent as a Jemez dancer
or the staff of a matachín.
It is a land of hunters
where men and animals
stand naked in a forest of light,
always taking aim,
always the target.

Between San Ysidro and Cuba
I come across a hunter,
a coyote killed by a truck in the night,
a spot of gore on the road.
His great head stands alone,
sculpture mounted on the desolate asphalt,
the jaws thrown open like the land,
the fangs bare to the immense sky.

This is his last and fitting comment
on the world of coyote,
the vast wilderness of death
he did not know
would fix forever in my heart
this final, silent, and classic howl.

Capulín rises, a perfect volcanic cone,
near Folsom, at the edge of the plains to the east.
We drive round the base in a pickup truck
hunting for deer, our tracks crisscrossing

the ghosts of cowboys on the Goodnight Trail,
Kiowas on their fast ponies, and earlier men
who hunted the mammoth and the great bison.
Capulín rises, a white marker
in a green and cloudy sea
while we, like cavemen, repeat the pattern below
before we, too, complete the circle
into memory, into silence, and into stone.

Looking down from Johnson mesa,
Ratón is a scattering of cold seeds of light,
mirror to the stars in the black sky.
I remember I am a fawn on this sheer ledge,
an early man wandered over from Folsom,
or from the cool caves at Altamira.
There is a cold wind sweeping around the rocks
as at Stonehenge, and through my bones.

Before my feet, a sharp drop falls
to the deer below nesting down for the night.
I remember that I am a tired hunter
and that time has caught me on this cliff.
There is nothing can be done for it
except let hunter and hunted sleep for a while.
Tomorrow we take up the chase again with the sun
here where the world breaks off,
snapped like a twig or a rifle shot
into the silence of the valley below.

Here the earth, too, is a hunter
restless on its trail through the void.
Driving on Highway 90
east from Silver City
crow crosses my path above San Lorenzo.
Gray squirrel does the same thing
in Gila Wilderness.
Halfway through Hillsboro
a whirl of cottonwood leaves
dances across the highway
following Percha Creek
down to Caballo Lake.
The Caballo Mountains to the east
rear up from the desert floor
shimmering in the afternoon heat,

horses trapped in stone;
much like unicorns,
they stretch their necks upward,
the great blue heads
neighing into the sky.

Rhythms of the hunt
demanding as the staff of the matachines
return to la plaza vieja de Alburquerque,
the boxes made of ink on paper.

Ya vienen los indios
de Guarecimé,
son los matachines
de Guarecimé

who come dancing with violins,
maracas, and their staffs
tapping old gypsy songs
on the hard-packed earth.

Ya vienen los indios
de Guarecimé,
son los matachines
de Guarecimé

with their crosses always
crossroads of Jesus and sinners,
vendors or popcorn and cotton candy,
miracle of water turning into wine

favorite miracle of winos
favorite miracle of poets.

Ya vienen los indios
de Guarecimé,
son los matachines
de Guarecimé

scaring the devil
the old Protestant devil
right back up
Martin Luther's bowels.

Ya vienen los indios
de Guarecimé,
son los matachines

de Guarecimé

weaving their cryptic patterns
during Holy Week in Seville,
solemn procession in Old Town
winding north up the Rio Grande

toward the Sangre de Cristo,
the matachines in the lead,
the matachines from Guarecimé
whirling in their minuet,

the matachines from Guarecimé
stirring up the sacred dust devils
from their desert graves to play
and dance to the scratchy violin.

Ya vienen los indios
de Guarecimé,
son los matachines
de Guarecimé

Son los matachines
de Guarecimé.
Son los matachines
de Guarecimé.

Words of ancestors
remembered a castle in County Cork,
a leprechaun hiding in the glen,
the clean taste of whiskey,
a beloved violin in the evening breeze.

A Victrola of the heart
plays in each box on the map
letting fly voices and words
which sing of another time.

A box on a map
is a whirling dust devil,
a ghost dance in ink.

Each box forms
a history of the flame word,
a cry from the past.

Ghosts walk arm in arm
around the Old Town plaza.

A pale tourist yawns.

Mr. Devine plays
a waltz on his violin.
Carried by the wind,

the music rising
from the bandstand in the square.
He dreams his children.

The old photograph
shows dark Irish eyes and hair.
He sees his grandson.

When she was young,
Rebecca Gutierrez sang
and danced in these streets.

Grandmother looks subdued.
Not at all like when she prayed
the endless rosary.

Another photograph,
family portrait, dated 1898.
Cristobal Mares,
patriarch of the family,
prosperous ranchero,
his eyes are the shade of history.
He remembers his grandfather's stories
about the long cattle drive
north from Guadalajara,
the throat-searing crossing
of la jornada del muerto
(the dead man's journey)
to arrive in the rio arriba country,
green mountains north of Santa Fe
then Taos and home.

Trinidad Pacheco de Mares
endures the eternal Taos winter,
the struggle etched in the set jaw,
the pursed lips.
She is the matriarch who bears
for her husband Cristobal six children:
Laureano, Porfiria, Isabel,
Fernando, Lupita, Eduardo—

my grandfather who is about fifteen
in this photograph, stubborn enough
to survive the loss of land,
the Great Depression,
slaving in the sweatshops
for the Santa Fe Railroad.

He will live long enough
to wrestle me as a child,
that strength of his still there
for me to draw from until now.

These Mares and Martinez stare
from the cold eye of winter
into the eye of the camera,
into the eye of death,
that bony-faced woman,
la huesuda, who smiles
and points her arrows at them
from my century,
from my eyes staring into theirs.
I turn away toward the future,
also found deep in the eyes
of David, as Goliath discovered

in a painting by Jaro Dedina.
David, confident as a man
delivered from the jaw of the lion
and from the paw of the bear,
ruddy and handsome,
his face the color of the earth,
takes up the foreground.
A visage as of a mighty power
to the right and above David's head
looks down from the sky
over the valley of Elah.
There seems to be no place
large enough on this canvas
for a Goliath to stand
against the steady gaze
of David's eyes.

Goliath,
seen only in the eyes of David,
sees a graceful motion not his own,

a dance he fears and cannot do.
For forty days
the Philistine came forward
large and clumsy as a doomed empire.
Morning and evening
he shouted defiance of the spirit.
Trapped now by these eyes,
his great bulk
reduced to pitiable smallness,
Goliath can do no thing
but murmur the ritual slogans
and lurch forward to the battle.

David's eyes will not let go.
Goliath, held fast to his footnote in history
by the eyes in this painting,
does not see the onrushing future,
the small stone
cast from the whirling sling of David.

A third photograph shows
my grandparents and their red brick house
on First Street in New Town.
It was the harsh thirties
and the photo tells
the old story of the Crash,
the land blowing away to Texas.
Grandpa is dressed in a cheap suit,
Grandma in what finery she could salvage.

Grandpa was bound
as my father was then bound,
hand and foot
by iron and steel and debt,
by the railroad "shops"
where men were sliced in half
by the indifferent tools.
The "shops," layered with grime,
so dark and gloomy
a worker could lean over a stairwell,
piss on the foreman below
and never get caught.

A train whistle
cuts from east to west

through a child's memory
that first flew and circled
high above some Andalusian plain,
or took flight on a fluted note
in the court of Texcoco.
Far away across the lake
and the floating gardens,
the ram's horn
called to yet another sacrifice.

The child cannot remember
what he remembers now
here in Old Town,
here with this map,
right here in the Rio Grande valley
where extinct volcanos
guard the west approach
and the Sandia Mountains to the east
sculpt the memories of stone age men.

Another camera has caught
the ghost in the KiMo Theatre.
Early 1930s, clean
New Mexico sky,
small town downtown Albuquerque
KiMo Theatre marquee:
Glen Tryon in *Hot Heels*,
Five Acts of Vaudeville.

Years later, Uncle Elfego
took me to see Roy Rogers,
Gene Autry, the Cisco Kid,
and all their epigones
who fought the good fight
against the ubiquitous bad guys.

Now, Uncle Elfego
sings in his grave.
Hot air balloons
float above Albuquerque,
balloons for his funeral
to rise with his spirit
and carry his memory into song.

Frozen, these figures

face the camera
to be caught in pure form.
The university student
dressed like a thirties dandy
raises his hand and salutes me
from his time to my own.

Another man, then in his 20s,
stares at me dumbfounded
from the west corner just north
of the old Fords and Chevies
on Fifth Street
more than half a century away.

The American afternoon crowd
in front of the KiMo
caught then by the camera lens
is now what it must be,
the frozen images within
the reduced and still life
dimensions of a photograph.

Three young businessmen
who try to sell arid mesa
and blue sky
greet each other.
The shadows of the distant future
cast by the camera
are too thin for them in this brilliant sun.

Too thin, also, for the heavy-set optimist
wearing the good suit
and smiling into the end of his era.
He stares like the last
black-and-white buffalo
into the dispassionate camera,
the last of his God-fearing kind.
He stands on the hood
of the Pierce Arrow.

Beside the Pierce Arrow
stands the happy baker from Lola's Cafe.
A woman and her daughter pause
to smile at me before they, too, exit
to their own half century.

Another Pierce Arrow continues east on Central,
black arrow crossing the bright day,
black arrow in black-and-white photograph,
black arrow crossing before my eyes.

It is New Mexico, late '20s or early'30s,
black-and-white photograph of the KiMo Theatre
appealing to the history minded

except for him, the ghost, the one who didn't pause
for the camera!
He's the fast-moving blur
him the clown,
sideshow barker,
seller of popcorn and cotton candy,
well dressed, it is plain to see
from the cloud puffs of form
which caught his hands
and sport coat sleeves,
also the pant legs and spats.
It is for him I sing—
him, the ghost
walking smartly along Central
to the El Fidel Hotel
or perhaps on to Old Town,
him, the ghost,
too slick to be caught by the camera,
too much to do
to be trapped by his own time.
Bones pass through his shadow
every day in Albuquerque.
Him, the ghost who stares at Uncle Elfego and me
in the KiMo Theatre
watching Gene Autry and Roy Rogers movies,
a shadow on an old photograph,
a hope solid but shapeless,
fleeting as faith.
Him, the ghost in the KiMo Theatre.

A train whistle echoes again
and is gone.
The train sits on a siding.
The rails turn into rust.
Weeds numerous as headstones

grow inside the roundhouse
crying like an old woman to herself,
longing for her dead children.
I am reminded of the whistle's
shrill lament,
the purpose-bound engine
coming down the tracks,
remorseless as memory.

To the west on the map,
Mr. McCarty's house
is the thick rectangle.
The square behind it
is the tin-roofed garage
where Donny McCarty showed me
how to parachute out of the attic.
It was our airplane
and it was our fortress
deep behind enemy lines,
our secret cave in a cliff
where our small bodies
became immortal shapes
of comic book and movie heroes.

Across the street
is the Manzano Day School
with its playground
open to the children
of the country club set.
We invaded that forbidden wonderland.
Once the watchman caught us,
Donny and me, talked of jail,
tossed us out of paradise
and warned us not to be caught there again,
warned us never to return.
I became an enemy of the state.

Nearby is the large square
meant to be Old Town Plaza.
The little domino on the north side
is the San Felipe Neri Church.
The other large square is the stone castle
Bernalillo County Court House of the 1880s
that became San Felipe School.

Every gloomy room held for a child
the ghost of an outlaw,
a cattle rustler, a hanged man.
The short leg of the L-shaped building
on San Felipe Street
is where I lived for one year
with good songs and a woman I dearly loved.

That thin rectangle on Lomas Boulevard,
New York Avenue, as it was called then,
stands for the word which is my center.
The bird of memory comes winging back
strong as my child lungs
gasping for air in an oxygen tent,
strong as the coal and cedar
in the wood-burning stove,
strong as the fresh-baked wild pheasant
my father hunted and killed,
strong as the July sun
across the worn linoleum floor,
strong as the outhouse stench
even in freezing December,
strong as the wind-and-rain-polished
adobe walls in the back yard
that stood broken and gaping,
strong as the horsehair and straw
mixed in those mud bricks,
strong as the vanished voices
that held together the singing vision.
On such wings
the bird of memory flies
and then falls back to earth,
to silence, to velorios,
to all the weeping women.

Where the map leaves off
there is a great white empty space,
the rest of the world.
Beyond Old Town, la Plaza Vieja,
the old women in black shawls,
the old fires turning to white ash,
there is only *terra incognita*.
I populate these boxes and lines
made of ink on paper

as best I can inside my head.
Then I turn away
to my own place and my own time.

El uncornio
malherido por estos tiempos
corre al margen del mapa.

Bajo la luna llena
las blancas abejas
labran panal de luz
en una noche serena.

He visto pasar el unicornio.
Hechizado, lo he seguido
a la margen del ancho mar.
No sé si me quedo

para siempre dormido
o al punto de despertar.
pero ya veo cristalizar
los granitos de sal
en el panal de las abejas.

The unicorn,
badly wounded by these times,
gallops along the margin of the map.

With the full moon above,
white bees
build a honeycomb of light
in the calm evening.

I have seen the unicorn pass by.
Spellbound, I have followed him
to the edge of the sea
where I know not if I sleep forever

or if I am about to wake.
Still, I see
the salt grains crystallize
in the honeycomb of the bees.

ON SIGNING AN AGREEMENT TO READ POETRY
AT A STATE UNIVERSITY

Great State University and
All your sage administrators:

You and I do enter into solemn covenant.
I swear I will not bring down on you
Labor difficulties, strikes, civil tumults,
Wars and epidemics.

Neither will I interrupt or delay
Transportation service, nor use
Salacious, abusive or obscene language,
Nor make obscene or offensive
Movements or gestures.

If, however, it should happen
That during the reading
The IWW musters its strength
And that One Great Big Union
Calls the last General Strike
of all the workers of the world

While, at the same time, Yeats' Great Beast
Slouches towards Bethlehem to be born
Amid floods, earthquakes, tornados,
Civil wars and dancing in the streets,

Then yea I say unto you as it is written:
Article 3 of the Lecture Agreement
And Clause 17 of the Standard
Entertainment Contract Rider
Shall be fulfilled.

You won't owe me a cent.
I won't try to collect.
If we find ourselves, afterward,
leaving town on the same freight train,
I won't look at you
And don't you look at me.

JUANA LA LOCA

I

Juana
que estaba loca
llevaba el ataúd
del cuerpo de Felipe
por muchos años.

Y tú
que no estás loca
¿cómo vas a llevar
el recuerdo mío
cuando te dejo?

II

Ella sabía
que sin Felipe
el agua se haría negra,
sucio el aire,
y la siembra se moriría
en el campo.

¿Quién le iba creer
en aquel entonces?
Hace quinientos años.
Todos pensaban
que estaba loca.

JUANA LA LOCA

I

Joanna
who was mad
carried Philip's body
in its coffin
for years.

You
who are not mad,
how will you carry
my memory
when I leave you?

II

She knew
without Philip
the water would turn black,
the air foul,
and the crops would die
in the fields.

Who
would have believed her?
It happened
five hundred years ago.
Everyone thought
she was crazy then.

SOME REFLECTIONS IN THE DESERT

The lizard reigns green and still
From his slab of lava rock.
He flicks a black tongue
And stares through me
With the flint-hard eyes
Of all his kin.

Green monarch
Of dust and baked earth,
I know the crunch of grit in my teeth,
The dry nudity of palm and fingertip,
And sand tasting of an acrid rust.

Mindless spotlight on lizard and man, the sun
Drives me inward from its merciless stare.
I seek water fountains, terraced gardens,
A blue forest, satyrs and nymphs.
Reptile, jump from your perch,
Go hide under a stone.

The lizard stares like a tiny sphinx
At this stranger in his realm.
Green lord of death and parched bone,
He ignores me from his throne.

THE SECOND COMING

—for Rudy Anaya

A hawk hovers over Albuquerque,
Drifting through choking air at the city's edge.
Confident in his own domain,
He is hunting for field mice
Scurrying through sagebrush
Along the west mesa
Falling away toward the Rio Grande.

He is hunting at the edge of history
Come full circle to the morning sun.
Now the hawk closes his wings,
Aims at the wounded beast city,
And dives in swift and final judgment.
His time has come again.

BOSQUE, NORTH VALLEY, ALBUQUERQUE

Winter Rio Grande, a slow trickle now,
Carries the melted snow down from the north.
Stands of cottonwood and scrub grass
Turn the bosque a wild ashen color.
The river is grey, springtime distant,
The bosque a tangle of vines sculpted by freezing wind.

I walk the east bank upstream toward Alameda.
Suddenly a coyote lopes ahead, stops and stares at me,
Then moves off into the camouflage undergrowth.
I cut away from him at a sharp angle
To the southward flow of water.

I think we carry pictures of each other
Inside our heads. We met once before
Beneath Sangre de Cristo peaks to the north.
Then our world was all fur and fang.
Now we part and go our separate ways
Along the Rio Grande, the Great River
Forming the dorsal column of our millennial voyage.
We will meet again. . . .

CLEOFES VIGIL

—in memoriam

Now the winds high above San Cristóbal
Carry his strong voice.

He sang the holy songs . . .
alabados . . .

He sang of ciboleros . . .
the long-gone buffalo hunters . . .

He sang of comancheros . . .
New Mexican traders

Who rode out on the staked plains
Where they mingled with Comanches.

And oh how he told stories
About ranchers and freight haulers

Who knew this austere, this stoic land.
Now when I drive the great interstates

Of Texas and Kansas, long before
New Mexico rises into view

Like a stark painting
By an anonymous village santero

I hear him singing . . .

Por los montes y los llanos,
Por los altos de San Cristóbal,

High above the plains,
High above San Cristóbal.

En los montes elevados
Está tu corazón.

En los montes elevados
Está tu corazón.

Adiós, Cleofes. Adiós, 'mano.
Que sigues cantando, cantando . . .

HORSES

Horses had to swim for it.
Dumped out of the Spanish galleons,
They had to keep their heads high
In the horse latitudes
(No social pretension here),
And make for the shore.

Horses galloped across the plains,
Not knowing they were mustangs
To be roped and saddled by
Two-legged creatures
We hold in high esteem.

Horses have names I can't forget.
Babieca who belonged to the Cid.
Trigger who belonged to Roy Rogers.
Bucephalus who belonged to Alexander the Great.
Rocinante who belonged to Don Quijote.
And there was Tony the Wonder Horse.

Horses belong only to themselves.
Once in the mountains north of Santa Fe
There were horses,
Descendants of Pegasus,
Who fled the rising snowdrifts.
Night and day without end, snow fell
On the upland mesas
And the horses moved higher and higher.
Soon no high ground was left.
The horses remembered their great wings
As best they could,
Stretched their necks up and pawed the wind.

When spring came and snow melted
Up there in the tall aspen and ponderosa,
Horses still flailed their hooves against the cold air.
The tree branches held them like offerings,
Stiff legged and eyes wide open, impaled,
Galloping at crazy angles to earth and sky.
The frozen horses filled my dreams.
Twentieth-century horses. Picasso horses.

Once a horse threw me and kicked me.
Another time, a horse made me sick with fever.
Thus they spoke to me of their deep hurt,
Their longing for the wings of old,
Their hatred of fences.

Stuck here in the human latitudes,
I'm learning to listen to horses,
To fear them less.
They talk of a world come full circle,
Earth broken and the waters poisoned.
You'd better swim for it, they say.

NEWS ITEM

—A valuable macaw escaped from his Old Town owner and has reportedly been flying about opening the cages of other macaws in the Albuquerque area. —Albuquerque Journal

The trappers came like common bounty hunters,
Or government troops moving against
Guerrilleros in the jungle.
They killed your mother before your eyes
And tossed you in a cage.
They did not know
Every breath you drew
Sucked in the atoms that once surged
Through Sandino, Guevara,
Zapata and Villa.

Caught and sold
Six thousand miles to the north,
You are placed on display,
A splendid jewel, a thing in a cage.
You remember the great thermals
Lifting your wings.
You bide your time
Until the cage door is ajar,
Then you swiftly and surely take wing.

Now, you fly with the kindred spirits of Popé,
The rebel Indians of long ago.
You fly the bright red banner of the IWW.
Everywhere the keepers of cages must cringe.

Nestle down safely in the bosque tonight.
Follow the Rio Grande south to your homeland.
The future flies with you.
You are a valuable macaw.
You open cages.

FLIGHT OF CROWS

—dedicated to Gilbert Merkx

These crows glide smoothly,
Always in one direction
Right to left
Across my field of vision.

They remind me of other crows
I have seen at other times,
Caw caw cawing black,
Wings flapping against the sky.

Not these crows.
Silent crows
Remorselessly black
As the absence of all light.

These are the nightmare crows,
The agents of oblivion
Scattered like black flack
Against the sky inside my mind.

Riding wings that stop time,
They are the harbinger crows,
The forerunners of total blindness.
They are the messengers of that bony-faced woman,

The old toothless one,
La huesuda,
The sightless hag
Who comes in majesty
Wrapped in her mantle of fog and night.

The silent crows glide
Right to left.
Then they are gone.

They will return.
They will return.

ONCE A MAN KNEW HIS NAME

*—dedicated to the memory of Popé,
leader of the Pueblo Revolt, 1640*

I

My name was ripe with summer,
A cornucopia overflowing with food
For the pueblos.

My name was the summer
Gathering together
The life-giving maize,
The plentiful squash, beans and chile
To feed the people of Oke Oweenge
And all the pueblos of our land.

As a child
I ran along the banks of the Rio Grande
And nibbled the sweet grass that grew there,
The blue grama, the little bluestem,
Camomile, and the sunflowers.

As a child
I learned the Tewa stories.
We came from beneath the Sandy Place Lake.
Our first mother was Blue Corn Woman,
The Summer Mother.
And our first mother was White Corn Maiden,
The Winter Mother.

All is sacred in our world:
Shimmering Mountain to the north.
Obsidian Covered Mountain to the west.
Turtle Mountain to the south.
Stone Man Mountain to the east.

All the hills are sacred.
All the shrines are sacred.
All the plazas are sacred.
All the dances are sacred.
All the directions and their colors.
All are sacred for the pueblo
The Spaniards called San Juan.

The Spaniard said our spirits were devils,
Their faith the one true faith.

In the name of God
They destroyed our kivas.
In the name of God
They burned our katchinas.
In the name of God
They forbade our dances.
In the name of God
They flogged our caciques.
When they took our Tewa names away,
Our mouths filled with the dust of our loss.

II

As a young man
I knew the colors of life.
I followed blue to the north
And my authority returned to me.

I followed red to the south,
Yellow to the west,
White to the east,
And my authority returned to me.

I visited the sacred hills and mountains.
I knew the Summer People.
I knew the Winter People.
I knew my own name.
My authority returned to me.

Then the Spaniards took me.
They flogged me.
They could not take away my name.
My authority returned to me.

At Taos Pueblo
Inside the kiva
I invoked P'ose Yemu,
He Who Scatters the Mist Before Him,
And my authority returned to me.

III

Then the war leaders came
And I spoke with authority.
I sent forth the runners
Bearing the knotted cords
To the two dozen pueblos,

To the six different languages,
To all the directions and their colors
From Taos to the Hopi villages.

When the time came
And the last knot unraveled,
We struck everywhere at once.
We raked a fire across the sun.

We let those Spaniards go
Who had lived with us in peace.
We drove the rest away.
We let them go.

When they returned with an army
Marching north to Santa Fe
I called upon P'ose Yemu,
He Who Scatters the Mist Before Him,
And the Rio Grande rose,
Breaking the marching ranks of soldiers,
Scattering the Spaniards
Into the mist along the river.

We broke their arrogance
Like bits of dry straw.
We drove them away.
We let them go.

IV

The Spaniards came back
And after a long time
Many of them became our compadres, our comadres.
Then all the others came.
We still endure.
We shine with the brilliance of stars.

Within and around the earth,
Within and around the hills,
Within and around the mountains
My authority flows
Like the waters
Through the pueblo lands.

I know my own name.
I know my own name.
I know my own name.

MAMA SNAKE

—for Keith Wilson

Paul turns and fires.
Paul and I target shooting on the mesa
then making our way back to the car.
Paul hears the rattler,
turns and fires, turns and fires.

Mama snake hears us coming
along her spine,
follows the message
crawl, crawl, get away fast,
curl up under the limestone ledge
wait there for the little ones
curled up inside their sacs,
inside mama
ready to add more of their kind to the world.

Paul turns and fires,
turns and fires in one motion.
Mama snake presses back into the ledge,
rattles going now, fangs bare
to the immense universe of hate.
Paul turns and fires.
Mama snake takes it in the middle.
Her head and tail go their separate ways.

Mama snake turns her dying head
to see what is left of her snake world,
the ruptured sacs,
seven baby snakes writhing up
out of blood and chaos,
snake dance of resurrection,
seven forked tongues on fire,
seven pairs of fangs.

Somewhere in my shattered heart
Paul turns and fires, turns and fires
point blank at mama snake
and from where her belly used to be
seven baby rattlers rise in snake glory
into the kingdom of snake.

IN THE SAN ANTONIO HOTEL

In the San Antonio Hotel,
Juárez, Mexico, Sunday night
At the bar I drink my tequila straight.

The bartender talks and he is a man
To be listened to. He has survived
Mexico and its transformations.

Díaz and the Positivists gave way
To Villa y la revolución.
He remembers wagon trains

Moving north from Chihuahua to Juárez,
And breadlines in Torreón.
During la revolución

He stood all night to buy bread
At five in the morning.
By six all the bread was gone.

Y la revolución? Well, it gave way to PRI
He says, and that is why we are here tonight
At the bar of the San Antonio Hotel.

The bartender talks his way
Back through the decades to his youth.
My mind's first photograph

Records the black hair, the sharp cheekbones,
Black fire opal eyes. Then the snapshots
Show softer features, grey and pudgy,

Many folds and wrinkles.
Now he has become something like resignation,
His eyes gone to grandfatherly gentle.

There are only three of us in the bar,
The bartender, another mexicano, and myself.
Later, back in my third-floor room

I throw open the window.
The green-and-red fluorescent sign
Of the Intermezzo Bar

Jabs me like a thumb in the eye.
My only companion for the night
Is a bottle of wine I brought from El Paso.

You must drink it, the bartender said,
Because you can't take it back across the border.
Outside the thick alcoholic moon

Coats the sky with a pale glaze,
An ambiguous border between dark and dawn.
I peer across the river to El Paso, USA,

The Rio Grande purling alone
In this space between two worlds.
A door slams and a car motor fades away.

There is a silence in my bones
And in the distance I hear
The lament of a slow-moving train.

FLOWERS AND SONGS OF SORROW

—reflections on three Aztec poems

I

We who enjoyed the festivals of flower and song . . .
We who now walk the asphalt streets
Named Londres, Hamburgo, Amberes, Liverpool . . .

We are beggars in rags
Who look with eyes alert at Mexicans and Americans
In three-piece suits and silk dresses.

We remember flowers and songs.
Once we were warriors and people of wisdom.
We remember flowers and songs.

II

Proud of itself
(Later came the broken spears
Lying in the roads)
The City of México-Tenochtitlán stood
Like an obsidian blade in the heart of Anahuac
(Later we tore our hair in grief).

Here no one feared death in war.
(The houses are roofless now, and their walls
Are red with blood.)
This city was our glory.

Worms swarm now in the streets and plazas
And the walls are spattered with gore.
The water has turned red, as if it were dyed
And when we drink it
It has the taste of brine.

Who could lay siege to Tenochtitlán?
Who could move the pillars of heaven?
We have pounded our hands in despair
For our inheritance, our city, is lost and dead.

We have chewed dry twigs and grasses.
We have filled our mouths with dust and bits of adobe.
We have eaten lizards, rats, and worms.

With our shields,
With our spears,
We were the defense of Mexico.
But we could not save it.

Flowers and songs of sorrow
Drift through the Plaza of Tlatlelolco
Where our people once danced and sang.

Yet the city exists.
From the vanished waters
México-Tenochtitlán rises.

III

This is what you are ordained to do,
Oh Giver of Life.
Bear it in mind, oh princes.
Do not forget it.

Remember, oh Giver of Life,
Our people to the north.
Remember those who are not Aztecs.

Remember those whose song
Is one of sorrow and hope.
Remember our people in Aztlán

We are the flowers of your colonias,
México-Tenochtitlán.
We sing the songs

With the voices of blind beggars.
We strum the broken guitars.

We play the flutes and harps
At the Temple of the Sun
And the Temple of the Moon in Teotihuacan.

We remember flowers and songs
Even when there is grief and suffering.
We remember flowers and songs.

Have you grown weary of your servants?
Are you angry with your servants
Oh Giver of Life?

We remember flowers and songs.
Festivals of flowers and songs.

EL PERRO MEXICANO

El perro mexicano
Tiene cara de brujo sabio.
Pequeño y harapiento,
Me sonríe
Como si entendiera
El latido de mi propia vida.

El perro mexicano
Aparece en la nieblina,
En la curva peligrosa
Del camino a San Juan Nuevo.
Tiene ojos tristes
Como las cruces que marcan
La mala suerte de algún desgraciado
Que manejó su carro aquí
Por última vez.

El perro mexicano
Me sigue en la plaza de Uruapan.
Viene cargado de largas historias
De cristeros y federales
Y sabe que no entiendo nada de eso.
Tiene la paciencia
De pasarse la vida sin hablar nunca
A una persona.
Me sigue, me sigue sonriendo,
Sin ladrar, sin esperanzas
Que van más allá
De un cariño o un hueso
Sabroso de cabrito.

El perro mexicano
Aparece en la tormenta
Cerca de Tingambato,
Rodeado de muchos muertos
De su tribu.
Entiende sin entender
Los sacrificios,
La pirámide
Con fuego en la cumbre.

Perro tolteca,
Perro azteca,

THE MEXICAN DOG

Looks like a wise wizard.
Small and ragged,
He smiles at me
As if he understood
The rhythms of my own life.

The Mexican dog
Appears in the mist
On the dangerous curve
Of the road to San Juan Nuevo.
His eyes are as sad
As the crosses
Along the road marking
The misfortune of someone
Who drove a car here
For the last time.

The Mexican dog
Follows me in the plaza of Uruapan.
He comes burdened by exhausting histories
Of cristeros and federales.
He knows I do not understand.
He has the patience
To live his life
Without ever speaking to anyone.

He follows me.
Smiling, he follows me
Without barking, without hope
Going beyond a pat on the head,
Or a goat's bone to gnaw on.

The Mexican dog
Appears in the storm
Near Tingambato,
Surrounded
By his dead kin.
He understands without understanding
The sacrifices,
The pyramid
With fire burning at the top.

Toltec dog,
Aztec dog,

Me mira
Con la sabiduría de su carne,
Sus pelos lacíos,
Sus huesitos artríticos,
Y me tiene lástima.

Ve que también soy animal
De carne y hueso,
De mirada perra
Por los siglos perros,
Por la historia perra,
Por las horas perras
Del fracaso.

El perro mexicano
Quizás no entiende
Nada de esto.
Pero sí me ve
Los aspectos de perro que tengo.
Nos hacemos amigos
Por un momento perro.

He looks at me
With the wisdom of his flesh,
His limp hair,
His arthritic bones.
He feels sorry for me.

He sees that I am also an animal
Of flesh and bone,
With the look of a dog
For the dog centuries,
For the dog history,
For the dog hours of defeat.

The Mexican dog
Understands, perhaps, nothing of this.
But he does notice
My dog qualities.
For one dog moment
We become friends.

THE DAY I FELL IN LOVE WITH JOSEPHINE EARP

—*for Patricia Clark Smith*

I was in Santa Fe looking at magazines
in the lobby newsstand of La Fonda Hotel
when I caught her eyes staring hard

from the cover of her biography.
Josephine Sarah Marcus Earp, the caption read,
photograph taken circa 1880. She reached out

from that shadowy print and caught me
with the curve of her breast and shoulder,
the high chin. Her sepia-tone smile

took me into an easy intimacy
unlike the time I ran my fingers
through the dusty tresses

of the skull of a long-dead woman
(the thin scraggle stuck at the temple bones)
and wondered what beauty once went there.

Here Josephine seemed a step or two away.
Her husband, Wyatt, would not approve
my covetous glance but he is safely dead.

What Wyatt cannot do will be done by time,
the fast draw who guns us down one by one.
For the moment now, I have my Josephine,

as impossible as any love must be.
When we embrace, the wind begins its song.
She's an undulant wave beneath the land

while I stumble on above.
We do an ancient dance around the sun.

ON READING IN A NEWSPAPER THAT I AM A STAR

I am a star
Although not of the first magnitude.

Now you've put this thing on me
So I have to watch out for every

Would-be star who comes drifting into town,
Dressed in black and riding a silver-saddled horse.

If you look up at the western sky at night
You will not find me there.

I'm too busy practicing
My fast draw, my quick burst of metaphor.
I only wanted to gather words
Out of the chaos, the darkness,

Compress them into light, however dim,
An offering to you for your many kindnesses.

Now I am only the possibility of quiet reflection.
Solitude is remote now, lifeless,

Much like the starfish washed up on shore.
All that is left is memory of form.

You who made me a star,
Don't expect me to put on the badge

Or become another Gary Cooper in *High Noon*
Mumbling about my duty,

Making philosophical comments
While I clean up the town.

Being a well-known poet in America
Is like being an obscure gunslinger.

Somewhere a fast-rhyme artist
Is hot on my trail with high hopes.

There's a grim rider riding after me.
His aim is straight. He never misses.

You might catch me on the late show
Riding hard out of town.

LA COQUETA

A true flirt,
She has so many names.
La huesuda, la flaca,
La calaca, la hedionda,
La tiznada, la fregada,
La tía Sebastiana
To name only a few.

In the market at Morelia
A young man running with a side of beef
Bumps into me.
The blood smears the back of my shirt.
I know that she is flirting again.
She's brushed up against me,
Left me a token of her esteem,
That bony-faced woman.

She knows I tried to find amulets
With her rictus smile
To hang from the rear-view mirror of my car.
She knows that at least I tried
To stuff her image into a morral
But that day she was not in the market.
That's why she smiled at me on the road
From Matehuala to San Luis Potosí
When the van hydroplaned out of control.
Pues no pasó nada.
¡N'hombre! No me digas.

She smiled again on the road
Between Guadalajara and Tepic
When I hydroplaned again in the Ford van,
Smashed against a guard rail,
Went hurtling across the road
Into the oncoming headlights.
This is it, I thought.
This is really it.
The oncoming headlights
Moved to the right,
Then vanished. No collision.
Oh, she had a good laugh that time.

I know we're on good terms,
That old flirt and me,
Esa pelona, cabrona, la desdentada,
La mala cara, la bribona,
La roñosa, la harapienta,
La chingada, la muerte,
Death with all her alluring names.

Come
Bony-Faced Woman,
Skinny One, Skull Face,
Bald-Headed One, Bitch,
Stinking One, Toothless One,
Soot-Covered One, Sour Face,
Screwed-Up One, Rascal,
Grim-Faced Aunt Sebastiana,
Ragged One, Dirty One,
Fucked-Up One,
Come, let us dance
On and on together,
Always laughing and dancing,
We're two of a kind.

CHRISTMAS AT THE HEALTH CARE CENTER
ON THE WEST MESA

My aunt is a wisp of curled hair,
Tiny cumulonimbus clouds circling
Her ninety years of life.

Outside, the contrails of great jets
Streak through the clear blue sky.
There is seldom snow in the singular

Motions of the winter of New Mexico.
Ah, but when the snow falls
It brings out the child to play!

We move toward some Christmas rendezvous
Now, each our own way as best we can
Across the nursing home landscape.

Her world bound now by the frontier
Of wheelchair to bed
And bed to wheelchair, my aunt

Dances round and round inside her head.
She dances back to the thirties and twenties
And says she loves me very much.

I give her a toy to pass the time.
It changes color to the touch.
Now she makes her own rainbows

As she talks of the small angels
Who sang all morning in choir
Moving from room to room.

My aunt chatters on and on.
She is dancing to some faraway desire
Caught up in her own deep song.

She is dancing toward the bright light.
She is dancing toward Bethlehem
Deep in the interior of the nursing home.

We hear off in the distance a ghost train
Whistling to a crescendo
Then fade, Doppler effect, into a moan.

I think of Van Gogh's whirling stars
Turning the dark to a blinding white,
Fred Astaire and his dazzling smile,

And for me there is no regret.
I hear great-grandfather's violin
Cracked and silenced a long time ago.

It plays the tunes he must have played
At weddings, funerals, gatherings like this.
Those songs are like the missing voices

From the old photograph in the album
All this is about to become.

'38 CHEVY

—for Frank McCulloch

Grey Albuquerque winter day,
Cold knifes through me
As sharp and harsh as sunlight
Blinding but no warmth.

I go into the Double Rainbow
For a sandwich and good coffee.
Frank has had that idea, too.
"Hey," he says, "have you seen my new car?"
"No," I say, "let's see."

Proud at the curb,
Elegant as grandma in her shawl
On her way to church to say the rosary,
The 1938 Chevy is splendid
In its black finish and red trim.

Surely a sign, I think,
From a bygone Route 66 Central Avenue
To remind me
I, too, still hit on all cylinders.
"Original paint and engine," says Frank.
"Y corre el cabrón.
I ran it at 60 mph to Bernalillo."

I stick my head inside
This car exactly my age
And catch the musty odor—
Ancient felt that has survived the decades.
The old Chevy is perched
Here, now, like a movie gangster's
Getaway car.

At the other end of my double rainbow,
Arching across the void
Into dreams and memory,
Are the last days of the Great Depression
And the nightmare of the fascist forties.

This '38 Chevy
Has survived the roll call of the dark decades,
The bombed-out roads, the ambushed detours,

The sharp curves, the dead ends,
The burnt-out bridges of this century.
It doesn't have a scratch,
Not one dent,
Is not, after all, an ugly duckling.

My rainbow arched up
From Woodie Guthrie songs
About Okies on their way to California,
With Route 66 so close
I could skim a rock over it.

My rainbow blazed with the songs
Of Pedro Infante and Jorge Negrete,
Mexican corridos,
Decades of Mexican restaurants
And the liquor stores, bars and cantinas more common
Than schools and churches in New Mexico:
La Cuevita, Red's Place, Okies, Jack's,
The Palms, The Tower, el San Miguel, Joe's Inn,
The Dew Drop Inn, La Ultima Copa,
El Madrid Lounge, the A Mi Gusto Bar.

That old Chevy and I
Have survived the dust devil that spun us around,
Shot us out here, at this end of the rainbow,
On a Friday Albuquerque winter day.

We pause, for just one moment
On this cold great divide
Between all that went before and all that
We will be: old paint, rust bucket,
Creaky springs, rocking chair writer,
Aching back painter.

No old folks home for us, no crazy quilt
Junk yards of sun-bleached dreams.
Like Bogart in the movies,
We are ready to tear out, brakes screeching,
In this '38 Chevy.

We repeat the migratory paths
Of old metal and bones,
'38 Chevy, Frank and me,
Back to ourselves,
Back to the deep song.
Corremos, cabrón. Corremos.

LUNCH AT THE GYROS

My head whirls
In the tender aroma of souvlaki,
Spanikopita and baklava.
Today Greek food in Albuquerque!

Tomorrow the world in a pita,
Or wrapped in a tortilla,
A true multicultural burrito,
Perhaps a spread for a pizza
Or bundled up inside a hero,
A po' boy dancing through the universe
Served with a giant Pepsi Cola
Bottled in Moscow!

Oh, it's a fine day!
A beautiful girl in tight jeans,
Her hair black as Apache tears
Hanging straight down
To where my eyes rest on her buttocks,
Orders falafel with tahini sauce.

I feel so good today,
I wish the politicians, bureaucrats,
And technocrats could have lunch
Here at the Gyros,
Come back to their senses
And go forth gyrating with the galaxy.
True believers beware!
I want to spin you off your feet,
Make you laugh at empty mirrors
In your dreams.

Come, have a good lunch.
Get your hands a little messy
Along with the rest of us
Here in this restaurant, the Gyros.

PAULA ANGEL

—*Paula Angel lived in turbulent late-
nineteenth-century Las Vegas, New Mexico.
She stabbed her brother-in-law to death
when he persisted in making unwanted
advances on her. She was tried for murder,
found guilty and sentenced to be hanged.
On the first attempt, she grabbed the rope
above her head, pulled herself up and
thwarted the hanging. However, a local
judge pointed out that according to the
law she had to be hanged by the neck until
dead. She was promptly hanged again.*

Paula Angel is a moaning wind
through the streets of Las Vegas.
Her long hair fills the mouths
of drunks who fight in the bars.
Her fingernails are the sharp knives
flashing in the streets of Las Vegas.

When the rafters of old Victorian homes
groan in the Las Vegas night
heavy with the weight of time,
it is Paula Angel, pulling,
pulling herself up
by the rope around her neck.

DISCOURSE OF THE SEVERED HEAD
OF JOAQUÍN MURIETA

—excerpt from the play, The Ballad of Joaquín Murieta,
first performed by La Compañía del Teatro de Alburquerque

From the waters of my mother's womb
I fell head first into the world.
I walked the land and came to know
The great beasts of the earth,

Also the lizard scurrying across sandstone,
The eagle and the hawk in the sky
And the ever-watchful buzzard.

Thieves and murderers
Severed my head, tore it
Like a ripe fruit
From a tree in full bloom
And dropped it here in this cold glass jar.

My head swirls in this filthy tomb.
I see the bleary-eyed drunkards at dawn.
I weep unseen tears in these waters
When I see myself through the eyes of drunkards.
I reach out with their leaden arms.
I stumble about on their uncertain legs.

Before I was twenty, I was as good as a Comanche
With a horse. My head thrown back,
My jaw open, I sucked in the wind
Until my lungs took on a wild ecstasy.
Now only dark waters flow into my mouth
And out again to this cloudy and closed sea.

With Carmelita I came to California
To work the mines of the land.
Here I found men more beasts than men.
Their blows drove me to the deep canyon
Where all rivers gathered and waited for me.
Now only dark waters flow into my mouth
And out again to this glass-bound sea.

My head turns and turns in this filthy jar.
I see the bleary-eyed drunkards at dawn.
Once my eyes caught the sun's fire

Burning through pine on a mountain ridge.
When Carmelita laughed, leaves shimmered
And even the doe paused in joy with her fawn.
Birds flew with a fluttering of wings.

Driven to the deep canyon, I became
The outlaw they wanted me to be.
Raiding through the California night,
With red-rimmed eyes I aimed and shot
My victims, the grim haters of life.

They forced me from the fields and the mines,
Violated Carmelita, then took my severed head
And let it fall like some broken bird
Into this miserable jar where it circles
Around and around in a dark and moldy sea.

DIALOGUE WITH A SKULL FOUND IN LAS VEGAS, NEW MEXICO

How does it feel
old skull bones with matted hair
to walk about again?

> The wind swirls through my eyes
> and through the caved-in bones
> where my nose used to be
> but I feel nothing.
> I don't even smell the bread
> fresh from the ovens.
> Are they still using the ovens?

Old skull bones, the ovens
have burned human flesh in our time.

> Your words cut through me
> as easily as the cold winter
> that took me long ago.
> Tell me, young skull bones,
> fat fleshed and full bearded,
> is your time more peaceful now?

It is a time of dreary violence,
as was your time. No offense, old timer,
but the sunlight pours beautifully
through the hole in your head.

> I survived that bullet.
> Only the years and the weather
> prevailed against me.

What can you say to me?

> I have learned the wisdom of silence.

You have no comments for the living?

> My eyes and my smile,
> which you cannot see,
> are the comments I make.

Are you Indio, Chicano, Hispano,
Mexicano or Anglo?

> I am starfire, windsong
> and clean bone.

Tell me, anciano, do you see at all?
Do you see in color or black and white?

> I see the colors of dream and memory.
> I see as a person staring from an old photograph
> into the lens of the ghost camera,
> into the eyes of the living.

Where does the photograph end,
old skull bones, and the image begin?
On the printed page or in the mind?

> When you look at a star,
> where does your vision end
> and the star begin?

ON A PHOTOGRAPH BY ALEX TRAUBE

Black horses
Light horse
Pinto in a snowy field

Winter horses
No rider will know you
As you are now

Six horses standing in snow
Forever now in memory
Near a fence and a road

Horses for a cold landscape
You stand now
Proud in your shaggy finery

Cold sentinels of dreams
You stand guard
Over all winter fields

Horses near Las Vegas
You stand like stone
Six icons carved by light

TRUSTING THE FIRE NOT TO GO OUT

Getting on to midnight
The old man and the old woman,
Dos viejitos,
Leave the bar.

He is blind and has a stick
To feel what is before him.
She is dim of eyesight but she leads
The way out into the dark.

He follows, confident,
That she knows the way.
She probes the air with her right hand
and her left guides him

By the coat lapel.
He uses the stick to avoid
The chair leg, to find

The door seal marking the boundary
Between in here and out there.
Once outside, it is pitch black.

They sense the starlight,
The flicker of dim points
On a map inside themselves.

She leads and he follows,
His stick flicking left and right,
Trusting the fire not to go out.

They walk on and on
Toward the fierce sun.

"Chulo here. I copy you."
His voice an old iron rasp
Dulled and gone to rust with time and drink,
Chulo downs another beer
Courtesy of the Plaza Tuxedo Bar.

"Chulo, shut up, these gentlemen
Don't want to listen to you,"
Says the owner of the bar.

"Oh yes, darling, I copy you,"
He says to her.
"I swing that broom
But now I go."

"Chulo, don't forget!
Be here by ten
To wash those windows.
And bring a ladder, you're so short.
Now get out.
You've had too much to drink!"

"I don't forget.
Chulo don't never forget.
Chulo here tomorrow morning.
Ten four."

"Hey Chulo, you like CBs man?"

"Oh yes! Chulo like CBs.
I talk to them rookies
All the time, man. You know,
Them smokies on the road.
I clean up Radio Shack
And I get that CB half price.
I be here in the morning.
Chulo don't forget.
Ten four."

Mrs. Martínez, the owner,
Tells the men at the bar
About Chulo and his twin brother,
How they got drunk together
And the cops would take them to jail.

"Inside the jail
They'd take their pants off.
Then they'd take turns
Hanging each other with their belts
Until the cops couldn't take it no more.
So they would let them go.

They were always together
Driving around in an old pickup truck,
Doing odd jobs.
Pobrecito, I feel sorry for Chulo."

"Last month Chulo got so drunk
He couldn't get across the Gallinas River,"
Says another man. "Every time he stood up
He kept falling back in the mud.
People stood around laughing.
Finally some kids helped him out,
Wrapped him in a blanket
And took him to his shack."

"What happened to the twin, Señora Martínez?"

"Well, about five years ago,
No . . . it's been longer,
Anyway, they found him
Hanging from a tree.
The cops said it was suicide.
When Chulo is very drunk
Sometimes he talks about how he and his brother
Used to hang each other."

Chulo's voice keeps coming back
From the nights I spent in the Plaza Tuxedo Bar:

"Chulo here. I copy you.
I got my own CB, man.
Chulo don't forget.
I copy you. Ten four."

THE ROAD TO FENTON LAKE

—for Carolyn Meyer

Directions become confused here
Where the road to Fenton Lake
Loops around the low crests

Near the cabin we loved.
Once below Redondo Peak
High in the Jemez Range

I worked my way toward the cabin
Down a switchback path
That zagged when I wanted to zig.

I remembered other times
When even a compass didn't help.
Like the time the blue norther

Came hurtling down the Texas plains
Or that impossible moment
I ascended a decorative staircase

Leading to a white brick wall.
It only happens in dreams,
You say, but I learned

The architect and I
Were caught in a stage prop
Conspiracy. I have lived

What the mathematicians call
Discontinuous curves or functions.
This time, however, I trusted

The road not to stop at a precipice;
The curve to be continuous, not decorative,
Not a desperate projection

Of some great need of mine
More real in here than out there.

And my trust was well placed.
You and the cabin were still there.

COMMAND PROMPT

My computer
reminds me of the elusive Trinity.
I say this

with no disrespect for theology
but rather because the metaphor
has its own intrigue.

God the Father is here, of course,
a lesser deity embodied
in the microprocessor.

The Son is akin
to the keyboard,
the source of the right code

necessary to gain entrance
into the ambiguous heaven,
the file with no name, the lost file.

And the CRT,
cathode ray tube,
reminds me so much

of the Holy Ghost
glowing with a cold flame,
institutional, remote

yet giving me the critical signals:
invalid file name, disk error,
command interpreter missing.

Finally there is the much-desired
command prompt that says "go,"
press on with your journey

through keys and codes
for you must become like a child
before you enter the kingdom.

POEM

—in memory of Jim Hall

There's a map of the high country,
Three dimensional,
Better than computer graphics

Imprinted on my own imagination.
City born and bred,
I am at heart a stone age man.

Mule deer who come down from the canyons
And through the ravines above the Río Chama
To feed upon the pasture at Ghost Ranch

Recall the mythic past.
I see the world through their eyes
When I drive through Abiquiu,

This land where the sun comes up in the west,
Then spreads its hues back to the east
Contrary to all logic and expectations.

Back with my own kind in the city,
I remember the deer,
Their luminous eyes,

The moon an obsidian mirror
Skimming over the Pedernal.
I begin to growl and grow fur.

With my new hooves
I paw the ground of the map inside my head.
I long for the ghost trail back to my self.

ELEGY FOR RAMON SENDER

As a child in Spain
He saw his friend electrocuted
While flying a kite
Beneath a sky made brilliant
By Halley's comet.

The comet was a kite and Sender
Held on to the string
As long as he could

Scornful of the state,
Old anarchist Sender held on
Through more than fifty novels,

Through the civil war,
Through the Nationalist columns
Advancing on Madrid,

Through Lister's Communists
Stopping the Fascist attacks,

Through firing squads killing
His wife and his friends.

When time swooped down like a kite,
Sender held on until he heard
The cante hondo of his own deep song,
The call of Seven Red Sundays

To return to primal things
(The fine dust of ash
To be scattered across the seas),

To write down at last
With his bones
The final Chronicle of Dawn.

Ramon Sender associated Halley's comet with the cycle of his own
life and death. In Spanish, *cometa* is the word for both kite and
comet. Among Sender's greatest novels were *Seven Red Sundays* and
The Chronicle of Dawn, itself a series of novels. The Spanish novelist
was for many years my esteemed mentor.

WATCHING OLD MOVIES

We sit in the darkened theater watching
Stars from our childhood move across the screen.

This is not like a VCR at home
Where the TV is too small in the den
And the dream is constantly shattered
By the ringing phone and the Doppler effect
Of sirens running up and down the street.
Off in the distance, always, a dog barks
Or two cats snarl at each other.

The old movies roll through our minds
Bringing back the great time
When we, too, were immortals striding this land.

Once the cave paintings at Altamira
Did the same thing for our ancestors,
Reminding them they had stolen fire from the gods.

We recall the Saturday matinee
At the KiMo or the Odeon Ritz, the dank
Odor of the carpets, the thick musk of popcorn,
The sticky texture of the floor where
Spilled Coke dried to a residue
That held on, not wanting us to come
Unstuck from childhood.

Now, once again, we reenact
The ceremony of celluloid,
The roll call of our bygone heroes.
First there were Roy Rogers and Gene Autry,
Then Gary Cooper and Bogart and Bergman,
Katherine Hepburn, Lauren Bacall,
Jean Tierney and all those
Beautiful women and handsome men,
Ghostly attractive in black and white
Or preternaturally vivid in early Technicolor.
The old movies were distant galaxies
Flooding our small towns and the weekend void
With starlight and song.

Then the movies were gone until next weekend
Like the great wheeling constellations
So near yet moving away from us

Lost forever in the distance, in the past.

We turn to each other in the dark,
Two flickering images caught in changing light.

We look again at the stars up there,
Their pale glow coming from far away.
We touch immortality for an hour or two.
We watch the old movie until it ends.

Stiff from sitting so long, we rise and stretch.
Vaguely diminished, we watch the credits roll by.
Then we leave slowly, as if under protest,
Reluctant to give back the fire to the gods.

ON AN EDWARD R. GONZALES DRAWING
OF A SANTA FE BAR, CIRCA 1940

Here is a drawing I value
For its very incompleteness,
For its altogether human
Lack of perfection.

Fading light/fading images:
The Spanish colonial chair
(Possibly from the nineteenth century)
Drawn here in tan pastel
(The only object with color)

Is realism's last gasp
View of this antique bar
(Also Spanish colonial)
Dominating the foreground
Of a den in a Santa Fe home.

Holy faith/holy place:
The candle on the left
Remains upright while its mate
Tilts at a modest angle

As if to say there was a party here,
Intimate but not really wild
Those many, many years ago.
The spigot on the gin dispenser
Has been dry for decades now.

The sketched-in image of another chair
On the left edge of the drawing
Recedes beyond memory into dreams.

Ornately carved shelves
At the back of the bar
Hold various decanters,
One possibly of Cointreau
(Although the label is vague)—
The smell of oranges still thick in the air.

Wooden candelabra hang from the ceiling
Above large flasks of wine.
One bottle rests on a barrel meant to be quaint
While others are scattered about.

These objects drawn from an old photograph,
Faint images in grey and black
(Save only for the tan chair)
Mirror the unfinished lives
These Santa Feans left behind years ago
Like banners unfurled and abandoned on the field.

They were lives very much like ours,
I suppose, as we try like them to hold on
As best we can with words, photographs, images
Of all sorts against the quick slide
Back to oblivion, to a world
Whose forms we do not know.

When Edward R. Gonzales saw how much I admired this particular
drawing, he gave it to me even though he protested that it was
incomplete and he was surprised that I did not want him to add more
detail to it. This poem is my expression of gratitude to Mr. Gonzales.

AFTERWORD

En *El poema del unicornio*, E. A. Mares consigue trazar un
amplio friso verbal en el que la geografía y la historia, la
tierra y el tiempo, la realidad y el mito, aparecen indisoluble,
mágicamente fundidos. No se trata de una tierra y de un
tiempo abstractos: se trata de Nuevo México y del tiempo del
hombre, de un hombre también concreto que puede ser el
propio poeta y muchos más hombres. El poema tiene algo de
elegía; es, en ciertos aspectos, una elegía serena,sin lágrimas,
en la que el dolor ante lo perdido está compensado, casi
hasta el punto de la ocultación, por un vigoroso aliento épico.
La realidad, la inmensa—en profundidad y extensión—realidad
a la que el poema alude está situada, o más bien recuperada,
en una zona fronteriza entre los recuerdos y los sueños: de
ahí la inesperada tonalidad lírica que tiñe incluso a los seres
y las cosas más prosaicas y cotidianas. El cruce o confrontación
de elementos distintos y hasta opuestos es constante: si lo
lírico se funde con lo épico, la carga meditativa que los versos
arrastran está configurada por el más hondo impulso del
sentimiento. La riqueza del poema se debe en parte a esos
contrastes y superposiciones: por un paisaje reconocible y
verdadero, descrito o recreado por E. A. Mares con admirable
intensidad y precisión, vemos cruzar el mítico perfil del
unicornio, símbolo de la belleza y de los sueños que el
hombre, tras crear, se complace en destruír. La reticiente
amargura que trasciende del poema está también compensada
por una insinuada esperanza: el unicornio perseguido y
herido encuentra—aunque sea en la marginación—una última
posibilidad de libertad y supervivencia.

AFTERWORD

In *The Unicorn Poem*, E. A. Mares succeeds in tracing an extensive verbal frieze. It is one in which geography and history, the earth and time, reality and myth, seem indissoluble, magically joined. This is not an abstract time or place: rather it is New Mexico and a man's time in it. This man, who is also concrete, may be the poet himself and many other men. The poem is something of an elegy; it is, in certain aspects, a serene elegy, without tears, in which the pain of what has been lost is compensated, almost to the point of being hidden, by a vigorous epic spirit. The immense reality, both in depth and in extension, to which the poem alludes is located, or rather recovered, in a frontier zone between memory and dreams: this is what gives the poem a surprising lyric tonality that colors even the most common and prosaic persons and events. The intersection or confrontation of distinct and even opposed elements is constant: if the lyric qualities blend with the epic, the meditative weight carried by the stanzas is shaped by the deepest impulses of feeling. The richness of the poem is due in part to those contrasts and combinations: moving across an accurate and recognizable landscape, described or recreated by E. A. Mares with admirable intensity and precision, we see the mythic profile of the unicorn, a symbol of beauty and dreams that man, after creating them, takes pleasure in destroying. The muted bitterness which emanates from the poem is also compensated by an implicit hope: the wounded and persecuted unicorn finds an ultimate possibility of liberty and survival, even if only as a marginalized entity.

—Angel Gonzalez